Wood On Wood
Ron Odrich
Clarinet & Bass Clarinet

CONTENTS

©2015 MMO Music Group, Inc. All rights reserved.
ISBN 978-1-941566-18-3

mmo

JAUNT

Jim Odrich

4

BRAZILIAN WOOD

Jim Odrich

BISQUEODOP

Jim Odrich

14

WALTZ

JIM ODRICH & RON ODRICH

WOOD ON WOOD

Gerry Mulligan

IDOL GOSSIP

GERRY MULLIGAN

24

MMO 3247

26

MMO 3247

27

MMO 3247

Music Minus One
50 Executive Boulevard • Elmsford, New York 10523-1325
914-592-1188 • e-mail: info@musicminusone.com
www.musicminusone.com

MMO 3247

ISBN 978-1-941566-18-3